Blooming in the Wilderness

Finding Peace And Contentment As A Single Person

Linda Herbert

Copyright © 2023 by Linda Herbert

Formatting and cover design by:
www.OpulentPress.com

Acknowledgements

My love and thanks go to all those who, through the years, have helped me gain a greater understanding of what it means to be a single person, and to reach a place of peace and contentment.

In relation to writing this book I'd like to thank Joe Benjamin for all his love, input, guidance and wise advice that he has given me along the way. And, of course, his wife Josie - and her love in supporting Joe, and me through it all. Also my thanks for taking the book on its final journey to publication!

My thanks also go to Gill Bough for all her love, support and prayer throughout the experience of writing another book, which is very different from the first one. And I especially want to thank her for her love and kindness in again taking on the task of proofreading this book for me; which I so appreciate.

Contents

Introduction

Who Am I?

Let me introduce myself, before I go any further..... My name is Linda (Herbert) and I have now, in the year of 2023, reached the age of 79 years old. I have never married, although I'm not saying that I never wanted to. I had no children of my own either, and remained single - what was commonly known when I was much younger - as being a 'spinster'! But I'm not holding my hands up to being a 'dried up old spinster' - which used to be another favourite term used!

I certainly didn't go through the early part of my life expecting to stay single. Nor did I go through the latter part of my life thinking: *"I'm single - that's what God's called me to be - so get on with it!"*

So - how did it all work out? What have I learned through these years and what has the Lord had planned and very patiently taught me?

Birds Eye View

Speaking from a 'birds eye view' I would say that I learned quite a lot in the earlier years about the feeling of frustration in myself, because I thought I wanted to be married and have children - but it just didn't seem to happen. And, alongside this, was the even greater frustration of pretty well everyone else thinking I should be getting married and have children - and who didn't hold back from making their feelings known.

As I grew older, and into my late 30's and into my 40's, it didn't seem to affect me so much. I believe this was probably because my walk / journey with the Lord grew deeper and I was more involved in wanting to walk with Him along the path that He was leading me forward on.

Then came my late 40's, through my 50's and 60's and I had so much else going on that I don't think I gave much thought to the fact that I was single! The Lord took me into a completely new season of my life as I went into my 70's and the subject didn't come to the surface again until more recently.

What I do know for sure is that my Father had it all planned out in detail - particularly those times when

I hadn't a clue about what was going on!

Father's Plan

So what was 'Father's Plan' for me? Well, like all of His children I didn't know in advance! As I've walked through the years with Him, He has unfolded it and revealed to me what He had planned - as and when He was ready to show me.

I've already given you a 'birds eye view' of my life as a single person, but trust you'll continue reading to find out more of the details of what my Father has taught me through the years about being single. I pray you'll find it encouraging, but also challenging - as I really believe we are very much in need of both in our lives..... We grow, through the challenges that the Lord takes us through, and we need to be encouraged to keep going through them and into a deeper relationship with Jesus. I also pray that you'll have open hearts and listening ears to hear what your Father wants to share with you in this season of your life.

CHAPTER 1

Early Expectations

Am I Willing?

It's rather an understatement to tell you it was somewhat of a shock when I first got asked this question….. Actually, I need to explain more about the question I was asked. The complete question, went like this…." Do you feel led to write something about your singleness, as an encouragement to others?". I was asked it in the June of 2022 - and why was it a shock? Let's just say that, at the age of 78, it's not really the question I thought I'd ever be asked!

Was I willing? To be completely honest - I'm not too sure that I was…. All I did know was that I couldn't say 'no' unless I'd checked it out with my Father! I did check it out, although I was pretty sure by then what the answer was going to be.... and the rest, as they say, is history - and here I am writing a book on being single.

Why Was I Asked the Question?

Before I get going on the nitty-gritty as it were - let me share a little more about how I came to be asked the question. Well, it actually arose out of another question, that I was asked back in the October of 2020, by the same person. The question being - "Did God ever reveal to you why your path did NOT include marriage and children?" - which was even more of a shock than the question in June 2022, concerning writing about it.

After I answered the question - I asked a question of my own, and enquired as to what had brought them to the point of asking me that question? I will in due course share with you the answers to these last two questions - but I'm afraid that it will be at a later stage in the book when that happens!

First I want us to look at what this book is really about: the state of being 'single', how it fits in with being 'married' - and how it all came about and resulted in being somewhat of a 'mess'......

In the Beginning - Adam is Lonely!

Adam - was the first human that God formed to live in the new world that He has created and brought into being! But we are told that God soon realises that Adam needs more company than just the animals, birds and all the living creatures that He's created for him to look after…..

18 Now the Lord God said, It is not good (sufficient, satisfactory) that the man should be alone; I will make him a helper meet (suitable, adapted, complementary) for him…..

21. And the Lord God caused a deep sleep to fall upon Adam; and while he slept, He took one of his ribs or a part of his side and closed up the [place with] flesh….

22. And the rib or part of his side…..He….made into a woman, and He brought her to the man. Genesis 2:18, 21, 22. AMPC

Adam's response was to say…..

23 …….This [creature] is now bone of my bones and flesh of my flesh; she shall be called Woman, because she was taken out of a man.

….and his immediate realisation was to comment that….

24 Therefore a man shall leave his father and his mother and shall become united and cleave to his wife, and they shall become one flesh. Genesis 2:23, 24 AMPC

God's Blueprint

So what we have been given to us here at the beginning of Genesis, is basically what God had in mind - a blueprint - when He originally created the human race. Within this is also, what is commonly called, the 'Biblical view of marriage'. The desire He had on His heart right from the beginning was for a man and a woman to share their lives and, together in love and harmony, produce offspring that, over a period of time, would populate the land that He had created.

It's important to also realise that, as part of His 'blueprint', God wanted to interact with mankind. Initially with Adam and Eve in the garden He had created for them to care for - and then with all those following after. And that's what actually happened to begin with - each day He would walk with Adam and Eve in the cool of the garden.

A Major Intrusion

I think most of us are aware that this idyllic setting - where Adam and Eve lived and shared their love with each other and with God - came to rather an abrupt end..... Eve, egged along by satan (in the form of a serpent) tasted the fruit (the one fruit in the garden that was forbidden - because it would bring them death) - and gave some to Adam as well, who also ate it.

7 Then the eyes of them both were opened, and they knew that they were naked; and they sewed fig leaves together and made themselves apron like girdles. Genesis 3:7 AMPC

You see, by eating the fruit of this particular tree - 'the tree of the knowledge of good and evil' - it was the end of their idyllic life in the garden.

8 ....they heard the sound of the Lord God walking in the garden in the cool of the day, and Adam and his wife hid themselves from the presence of the Lord God among the trees of the garden. Genesis 3:8 AMPC

The End of the Garden

After this both Adam and Eve were sent out of the garden.....

23. Therefore the Lord God sent him forth from the Garden of Eden to till the ground from which he was taken. Genesis 3:23 AMPC

Essentially they became the first 'farmers' in the land, and also started their family!

God's Intention

It would seem that God's intention right from the start was that men and women should be together in a love relationship. That out of that relationship would come offspring and, over time, the human race would grow in numbers and spread over the earth that He had created.

When Eve, and then Adam, ate the forbidden fruit - did it change / nullify God's original intention for mankind? No, I don't believe it did! Yes, there were changes - but only in order to fulfil His intentions and overcome the obstacles preventing the outcome to His plan. God's answer was brought about through Jesus - and we'll see how this came about as we go forward.

God's Desire

At the core of all that's happened since the disobedience that occurred in the garden - lies the desire of God's heart…. to live in a love relationship with those He has created. And, alongside that, for those He has created to live in a love relationship with one another.

The Situation Today

So…. what is the situation that we find ourselves in today? God has given us free will and we, each one of us have the choice as to whether we walk in His way of doing things - or choose to go our own way. Basically, we can choose to follow the 'blueprint' God has given - or not, as the case may be.

What I believe we've ended up with - is partial understanding of God's way; partial willingness to follow His blueprint; and partial action on the part of mankind in general. And this has resulted in a great deal of confusion! Especially as, in amongst it all, are those who are wholehearted in following God's way. Many are still confused on how that should be carried out in regards to marriage and where on earth does being 'single' enter into it all - if it does?

Expectations

The whole 'expectation' of marriage plays a large part in this because, universally, I think the majority of us grow up surrounded with this expectation within both our families and society in general. This is especially true in respect to girls - and, in many ways, gives them a false outlook on being adults. This whole 'expectation' of getting married is very much the 'norm', particularly amongst the 'teens and 20's' age group - and the majority of those around you at that age also seem to expect it.

It's also true to say that, in many of the cultures around the world, the pressure of being married is even greater than it is in western culture. It was viewed at one point that 'marriage' was the only role in which the females of the human race could find their place. This has eased greatly through the years - but there is still tremendous pressure for girls / women to become wives first and foremost.

Growing Up

I was born in the '40's, so I was growing up as a teenager in the '50's and in my twenties in the '60's! I don't think that myself, or the girl friends I had at school, had any intentions of doing anything else but getting married and having children - as soon as we were old enough to do so..... And, to be honest, I can't remember hearing anything from anyone to suggest that we would be doing anything else.

Obviously we were aware that there were some single people 'out there'. You'd hear people refer to their 'maiden aunt'; or people would mention someone - and then tag them as being a spinster or even, if they were older and maybe a bit crabby, as being a 'dried up old spinster'. But the references wouldn't be dwelt on and, very definitely, it wasn't something or someone that any of us would become! You could describe it as the innocence but, at the same time, the cruelty of youth.....

This mainly continued as I entered my '20's but, of course as I grew older - I came across more single people. Some of them seemed reasonably happy in their single state - but I found many of them still very much 'on the hunt' to find someone to marry - and, to be honest, at that point so was I!

A Different Way of Thinking?

For me personally, something happened in my life to begin to change my thinking somewhat - although, looking back, I think it should probably have made much more of an impact than I allowed it to. Was this because of the way things were viewed by the majority....? I hope to look more closely at that question later.

So.... what happened to start to change my way of thinking? When I'd not long turned 20 in 1964 - my life changed direction completely, and nothing was ever the same..... Don't worry - it was a change for the 'good', which I've never regretted making. I had the opportunity, which I took, to commit my life to Jesus - and He came to live in me! And 'no' - I didn't become 'religious'.... what I set out on and began, the evening I made this commitment, was to enter into a relationship with Jesus - and I've walked with Him through everything that's happened in my life since then - the good and the bad!

Now I found myself in the position whereby I still had the same surroundings and views around me but, into the mix, had been thrown another part of the equation. What actually was the right view for a born again believer to hold? And, believe me, that turned out to be a very difficult answer to track down.....

A Learning Curve

So what in fact did I learn out of all this? I think I can probably say that, at the time, I found it very difficult to learn anything very much. What was very obvious was that people were very rigid in their thinking on the whole subject of marriage being for everyone - and being single didn't really enter into it!

Looking back to that time now, and realising what the Lord has taught me - I view it very differently, which is precisely why I'm writing this book! I want to share with you some of the things the Lord has taught and shown me through the years, and pray that it might help someone else to see things differently. Most of all that it might help to, not only 'see' things differently, but to 'act' differently and not experience the heartache that many people go through in this area of their lives. And some of whom, I'd venture to say, are never really healed in their emotions.

On the technical devices that the majority of us have as an integral part of our lives - if things aren't functioning correctly, we take steps to put them right! Sometimes we have to use the 'reset' button to return them to their 'default setting' - ie to the way the creator of the device intended them to work originally.

I believe, as born again believers, that we have been 'reset' to enter into the life that God originally intended when He created us. Unfortunately, it doesn't happen all in one go, as it does with a device - but it's the beginning of the process. Changing our thinking in regard to marriage and being single is a vital part of this process (reset) - and is an important part of growth in our relationship with the Lord.

I'm trusting the Lord to show us more about this, as we go forward....

CHAPTER 2

Reality Sets In

God's View on Being Single

As we saw in the first chapter, God's original 'blueprint' and the desire He had in His heart right from the beginning, was for a man and a woman to share their lives and, together in love and harmony, produce offspring that, over a period of time, would populate the land that He had created. An important part of this desire was His ability to be able to interact with His creation - and, initially, that's exactly what He did, when He would walk with Adam and Eve in the garden in the cool of day.

But, when sin and death entered into creation

through the beguiling of Eve by the serpent, things began to change. This is basically why there is such a confused view of marriage, remaining single - and all the various 'shades' between. And again, as we saw in the first chapter, this is as prevalent within the church as it is within the 'world'

What took place in the Garden of Eden definitely brought about a drastic change in God's original blueprint of the male and female species of mankind coming together - it would seem that God hadn't catered for single people as such. I wonder if that's why throughout history the majority of those not married were looked down upon?

But is that / or was that God's view? No, I don't believe for one moment that was the case - it wouldn't be possible for our loving Father to take that view, He loves each and every one of us, whether we acknowledge it or not!

What Does the Word tell Us

We did briefly look at the biblical view of marriage (God's blueprint) in the first chapter but, don't forget, that was prior to everything being disrupted by the enemy and what happened in the Garden of Eden. We also said that the blueprint on God's heart didn't change or, in fact, wasn't 'amended' as such but, I do believe it was added to. In view of all that happened, I believe our Father made provision for those who would end up being in the 'single' state. In fact, Paul has a lot to say in the New Testament about this.

But I'm jumping the gun a bit, as we need to look in more depth at what this chapter is examining. We're looking here at single people - looking at the reality setting in of the possibility of remaining single - when everything in them is saying they should marry and have children. And pretty well everyone around them is saying the same thing and expecting that to be the case!

A Single Person's Outlook

We're mainly looking in this section at the 'outlook' of a person who has never married but, many aspects can be also attributed to those who are widowed or divorced. I believe a person growing up in a Christian home, with parents and family who are believers - would be fully versed in what the Word says about marriage. I doubt that anything very much would have been said about 'not' being married and, in their early years, it probably hadn't occurred to them that they might not actually meet up with someone, marry and work together in God's Kingdom.

How Do I Find My Way Through the Maze?

I want to look more closely at the 'questions' someone faces, who begins to realise that nothing seems to be happening on the marriage front. I want to liken it to being faced with a 'maze' which I don't know how to get through. First I'm going to look at it from the point of view of continually finding a 'dead end'…. Then in the next chapter, entitled "What Now?" - I'm going to look at how to find the way through to the centre of the maze and make a start on making sense of it all. Included in that will be to look at the questions raised by the various paths ventured along and the possible answers…..

Obviously I can't speak for all the single people who will read this, who might say "That's nothing like my experience!" But, and I'm praying this will be the case, many of you reading this will find you can at least identify with some of what I'm sharing….

Why Me?

Did it mean I had failed in some way because I hadn't married? To be honest I think there were times when I felt a bit like that! My basic thinking began to change when I was born again into the Kingdom of God and I learned about 'Biblical Marriage'. That's when I began to see from the Word, and believe in my heart, that God would help me find the partner of His choice. But as time passed by and the 'partner' never materialised - I began to be even more confused and, looking back, it did actually feel a bit as though I'd taken the wrong turning in the maze! Especially when most of the people around me of roughly my age were either already married, or well on the way to being - which resulted in me attending a good few weddings and raising the question "Why them? Why not me?" Not helpful!

When the 'Hunt' Takes Over

So let's try another path in the maze..... And, amazing as I find it now, I travelled down this path twice - both ending up as dead ends. The first time was when I was in a smallish fellowship up in the midlands; the second when I was in a much bigger fellowship in the south London area - the one actually, where a lot of weddings took place. "What happened?" you've a perfect right to ask.... Very little really, outside of what went on in my own head!

To be completely honest, I don't think the male concerned in either case, had any idea of what was going on in my head - and I do thank the Lord for that. Why twice? I believe, looking back now, I 'went round the mountain' twice - because I didn't allow myself to learn the lesson the first time! Did other people realise? To be honest, I don't really know - I have to say "I hope not!"

In both cases I met the men concerned through the church fellowship I was part of. I liked them and begun to wonder if this was the Lord bringing me in contact with them. In both instances I realise now I began to put a 'case' together - that was entirely of my own making, and nothing to do with the Lord at all. Over time I began to realise what had happened - realising also that neither of the two men involved, although they knew the Lord, didn't seem to hold Him first in their lives. I realise now that my Father loved me enough to make sure I went no further in what, after all, was my fantasy and definitely not His plan.

My experience in going down that 'path' - poses two questions: "Do some people marry simply for the sake of proving they can catch someone?" Or another question which asks - "Do people (themselves and those around them) view success as getting married and having children?

Men In My Life

Another 'path' in our 'maze' takes us to the question: "If I don't marry - what part do / will men play in my life?" A question, in fact, that could stir up all sorts of issues as we try to look at some of the 'questions' raised on these different paths that we've ventured along!

Left Holding the Baby!

I feel I need to also look at another possible 'dead-end path' in this maze that we're trying to get through - the desperate lengths that desperate people will go to. Biblically it's made clear in the Word that we 'save' ourselves for the 'husband / mate' that God has chosen for us. But what happens when a person gets so desperate to have a child - even if they don't eventually end up with the father of their child? This is definitely not the route of a born again believer, more of someone in the 'world', but a person's outlook so often becomes blurred and confused - and desperation can produce very different results....

Pretending To Be Happy I'm Single....

And, I guess the final 'path' I want to explore is the one when a person realises their single state is more than likely be long term. They aren't happy about it, but pretend they are.... in spite of already knowing the path is definitely a dead end!

Where To Go Next?

Having looked at several dead-end paths, none of which have given us answers - where on earth do we go next? The title of the next chapter is "What Now?". We are going to tackle that exact question. We will start to see how we can go forwards - past the 'dead-ends' that the enemy has led us on; into what our Father says about it all..... and what exactly His plan for us is all about.

CHAPTER 3

What Now?

The Need For Honesty

Having been down so many 'dead-end paths' in the 'maze' (and I'm pretty sure there are even more than the ones we've looked at!) - it's no wonder that we've reached the stage of asking the question "What Now?"..... And, if we're going to come to any sort of conclusion at all and get to the centre of this maze - then we need to realise that we need to be honest with ourselves about the situation we find ourselves in and, most of all, honest with the Lord and what He is saying to us about it all. The second part of that last sentence we'll mainly look at in our fourth chapter - but, prior to that, we need to look at where we are - and make sure we're 'looking' honestly!

The Need to Know What the Word Says

As well as our need to be honest with ourselves - we also need to remind ourselves what the Word says. We don't necessarily find specific verses about the situation, but I would like to point our thoughts in the direction of how we need to manage our thinking about it all. In other words - our 'mind-set'.

5 Trust in the Lord with all your heart, And lean not on your own understanding;

6 In all your ways acknowledge Him, And He shall direct your paths. Proverbs 3:5-6 NKJV

And the Message translation really hits the nail on the head.....

5 Trust God from the bottom of your heart; don't try to figure out everything on your own.

6 Listen for God's voice in everything you do, everywhere you go; he's the one who will keep you on track. Proverbs 3:5-6 MSG

Those of you familiar with the Word will realise this is just a mere 'taster' - in other words there is a great deal in the Word to lead and guide us in our attitude and thinking, not just on this subject we're looking at, but on so many aspects of our day to day walk with the Lord. But that only ever applies if we're willing to find out what He has to say on the particular challenges that we're facing - and to be honest with ourselves as to what He's saying to us.

I should clarify that we're not looking yet at what the Word says specifically about being single as opposed to being married. We're looking at how the Word guides us when we find ourselves in the sort of situations resulting from going along the various paths in the maze and not finding what we want! The emphasis being just that - what 'we' want, as opposed to what 'God' wants for us!

The 'Paths' We've Tried

Now I want us to look more closely at the different paths that might have been tried by you - and some of the questions raised by them. At the same time, I want to see if we can find out what the Word says and what the Lord might be saying concerning them.... But, prior to that, I have to be honest and admit that, at the time of asking myself the questions - I wasn't really in a place in my walk with the Lord to actually ask Him or, to have necessarily accepted an answer. My hope and prayer is that, some of you, reading this book may be helped with the challenges that these 'paths' bring. I haven't been along all the paths, but will share my own experience of the ones I have - and ask the Lord to show me what I can share about those I haven't been on.

The "Why Me?" Path

This was the first path - when I was looking at all my friends getting married, but nothing was happening with me! For me it raised the question as to "How long do I go on trusting God for a partner?"

In Jeremiah the Word very clearly states that:

11 For I know the thoughts and plans that I have for you, says the Lord, thoughts and plans for welfare and peace and not for evil, to give you hope in your final outcome. Jeremiah 29:11 AMPC

Unfortunately, I only asked the question "Why Me"? of myself - I didn't ask God…..!

The 'Hunt' Takes Over Path

In the previous chapter I shared with you that I, unbelievably, actually went down this path twice at different times in my life. There was possibly a small, very small, element of asking the Lord about it but, basically, I listened to my own answers (which I had all mapped out!) rather than finding out from Him what He was saying to me in the situation….

I think the first question that arose in me as a result was "Do some people marry simply for the sake of proving, to themselves and others, that they can 'catch' someone?". Definitely not the way the Lord works in our lives. And following on from that I found myself asking this question as well…. "Do people (themselves and those around them) view success as getting married and having children?"

I think I'm going to return to the Message translation on this one….

6 ……don't try to figure out everything on your own. Listen for God's voice in everything you do, everywhere you go; he's the one who will keep you on track. Proverbs 3:6 MSG

I don't know about you, but I do know I'm very good at deceiving myself about things - which means that it's even more important that I really listen to what my Father has to say about it all. I am glad to be able to say that, all these years later - and the changes He's made in me, I'm more honest with myself - and more honest with Him!

The Men in My Life Path

I didn't say a great deal about this in the previous chapter, mainly just the question that arose in me: "If I don't marry - what part do / will men play in my life?" This was because I want to explore it more fully in the final chapter when we will look at, what I believe is the answer. I could comment more on the question but don't feel it necessary at this stage.

Left Holding the Baby! Path

Some single people desire so much to be in a relationship and have children, that they can get desperate and end up pregnant. This can then lead to them being left to bring up a child on their own - or often ending up in a toxic relationship.

This isn't a path I travelled down - but I can understand how some get led into this dead-end path.....

Again the vital ingredient is so often missing - if only we would ask God to show us and seek an answer for our situation in the Word.

If we honestly want to know His answer - He'll always show us.....

105 Your word is a lamp to my feet and a light to my path. Psalm 119:105 AMPC

The Last Path - Pretending To Be Happy That I'm Single....

I wonder how many of you reading this have reached the point of concluding that you're more than likely going to stay single - although you're not happy about it....? What is going to be your attitude about the situation, I wonder. Will you be honest about it and admit that it's not what you want - or will you do a 'cover up' and pretend you're perfectly content with it being the case?

This isn't a path I travelled down but I can quite see that, in some respects, it's easier to say you're 'ok' with it than to say you are not! My Father took me on a completely different path on being content with being single - which I will share later. One that, actually, I didn't fully realise until quite recently in fact.

Finding the Path to the Centre

Well, we've looked at a variety of dead-end paths in this maze we face as we walk the 'single' way, and I would imagine that most of you could tell me others that you've been down! However, what we really need to find out is HOW we get ourselves to the centre of the maze, where we're going to find the KEY to it all.....

CHAPTER 4

The Key to It All

What God Says - About Marriage

We talked in the first chapter about what God had planned for the first man and woman He created and how His 'Blueprint' had to be changed through the successful intrusion of the enemy into the Garden. We looked at how the blueprint itself remained unchanged - but we realised that additions were made to cater for the fact that some may end up without life partners, and what affect this would have on mankind.

What God Says - About Being Single

At the start of the second chapter we acknowledged that, in view of the success of the enemy with Adam and Eve in the garden - God made additional provision for those who would end up living the single life. And I said we would look in more detail at what the Word says about this - and we will.

How Did God Solve the Problem?

By this question, I'm asking how God put things right and kept everything on track to accomplish His original intention, when it seemed it had been hijacked by the enemy?

When the enemy (ie satan) successfully persuaded Eve to eat the forbidden fruit; and she, in turn, got Adam to join her - the result was that 'sin' ('death' in fact) had access to mankind and entered into the equation. The ONLY way that God was able to put this right, and reverse it, was this: He sent His Son, blameless and without sin, to die on the cross at Calvary and rectify the situation for each one of us.

However, because we ALL, every single one of us, have been given free will and are definitely not created as 'robots' - every single one of us has the choice as to whether we accept what Jesus did for us..... We have to choose - and no one else can make the choice for us.

But, you ask, 'why' and 'how' does this solve the problem? The 'why' is because Jesus bore our sin on the cross and we don't have to provide an answer for ourselves. The 'how' is through us accepting what Jesus did for us and asking Him into our lives.

The Centre of the Maze

Choosing to ask Jesus into our lives is actually only the beginning - that is how we arrive at the centre of the 'maze'. But that's when we begin to live our life in relationship with Him and, what happens from there onwards, is very much dependent on how that relationship develops. Remember, it was when Adam and Eve were disobedient to what God had asked of them, that their relationship with Him initially broke down. And the same is true of us. I believe that's possibly why so many of God's children face difficulties in their relationships, whether in marriage or otherwise - their relationship with God is not central in their lives. I'm not just speaking from what I've observed, but from my own, personal experience and will share more about this in the next chapter.

God's View On Being Single

Before going any further - I want us to look at what the Word says about being single. Many people seem to take the view that, ending up as a single person, is a form of punishment from God. But that's not what the Word says. Actually the Word says that 'singleness is a gift'.

This is what Paul says about it....

7 Sometimes I wish everyone were single like me—a simpler life in many ways! But celibacy is not for everyone any more than marriage is. God gives the gift of the single life to some, the gift of the married life to others. 1 Corinthians 7:7 MSG

But Paul was also realistic, and continues....

8 I do, though, tell the unmarried and widows that singleness might well be the best thing for them, as it has been for me.

9 But if they can't manage their desires and emotions, they should by all means go ahead and get married. The difficulties of marriage are preferable by far to a sexually tortured life as a single." 1 Corinthians 7:8-9 MSG

Your response to this might be that it's Paul speaking and not God! However, let me share what Jesus Himself said in Matthew.....

11 Not everyone is meant to remain single—only those whom God gives grace to be unmarried.

12 For some are born to celibacy; others have been made eunuchs by others. And there are some who have chosen to live in celibacy for the sacred purpose of heaven's kingdom realm. Let those who can, accept this truth for themselves." Matthew 19:11-12 TPT

And to underline it - as given in the Message translation....

11 But Jesus said, "Not everyone is mature enough to live a married life. It requires a certain aptitude and grace. Marriage isn't for everyone.

12 Some, from birth seemingly, never give marriage a thought. Others never get asked–or accepted. And some decide not to get married for kingdom reasons. But if you're capable of growing into the largeness of marriage, do it." Matthew 19:11-12 MSG

How Do We Choose?

I have no intention of labouring the point concerning choosing between being married or being single. But I'm coming to the conclusion that our biggest mistake is to approach it from the wrong direction…. with the question "How Do *We* Choose?" actually being the wrong question to ask!! The word 'we' being completely the wrong word to be at the centre of it.

And I can almost hear you asking "Why?"…….

WHO Should Be Choosing?

This is the question I realise I should have been asking all those years ago, when I was at an age when I was wondering if I would ever meet anyone and marry them. The time when I was exploring the different paths in the 'maze' and trying to work it out. Never realising that the *'key'* to it all was my relationship with **Jesus** - and that He had the **Answer**!

It's not a question of 'we' (that's you or me) at all in making the choice. It's actually a choice made by Jesus - the One Who created us and planned our lives out of His great love for us. He is the ONLY One Who knows what is the best for each one of us.

JESUS is CENTRAL To It All

God made a way through Jesus, that each and every one of us can live a life that fully satisfies - whether it's in marriage or as a single person (never married) / a widow or widower / or a divorcee.

It's easy to take the view that if you're not married you'll be lonely. But the well-known minister, Nicky Gumbel, speaking about loneliness tells us that: "God does not intend for you to be lonely and isolated. Loneliness has been described as 'a homesickness for God'. God created you for community – calling you into a loving relationship with Him and with other human beings." And I would add that the relationship with 'other human beings' refers to both married and single!

Remember, we have the choice about what we think about and in this situation we see again the importance of making sure we have the right 'mind-set' concerning it all.....

CHAPTER 5

Working It Out

My First Step Towards the Centre of the Maze

The first proper step that I took towards finding my way to the centre of the 'maze', where I would find my answer concerning being single, took place in 1964, not long after my 20th birthday. You may remember me sharing this with you, in the first chapter of the book, when I shared how my life changed completely for the better.

I also shared with you this thought (easier for me to share it again - than to send you back to look for it!):

"Now I found myself in the position whereby I still had the same

surroundings and views around me but, into the mix, had been thrown another part of the equation. What actually was the right view for a born again believer to hold? And, believe me, that turned out to be a very difficult answer to track down....."

To be honest I never really found anyone who was single, who could fully satisfy me with an answer as to the right view for a born again believer to hold in regards to being single. Nor how you managed to obtain it - although I realise, and admit that I should have taken more notice of what Paul said! I was given the 'right view' by one or two dear friends - but they were married and, unfortunately, I wasn't in a place in my relationship with the Lord to take it on board. Not in the same way that I would have done if someone who was single had shared it!

As I'm writing this now - I've a sneaky feeling that that is maybe one of the reasons why my Father has brought me to the point of writing this book......

Wrong and Right Steps

In the third chapter we looked at the various paths that turned out to be a dead-end, with some of them being ones that I had tried out.

There was one question that arose from the path concerning "Men in My Life?", that I promised to look at more deeply in this chapter. I do believe that it's important that, as single women, we have men in our lives and, I can almost hear you already asking "How on earth do we go about working that one out?"

We don't, and we aren't able to make those connections that we need with the right men to be a part of our lives, as we go forward as single women. But God can - and He will, because He knows how important it is and He created us in the beginning to be partners with each other.

I'm not so much aware of this being the case in the early days of my journey walking through life with the Lord. But, as I grew older and probably less likely to meet the 'man' I hoped to - this is what happened, although I'm not sure I was aware of it much at the time. Looking back now I realise that the Lord brought strong, loving men into my life (albeit married!) that loved and walked with Him, and who looked out for me and guided me.

If you are a single woman reading this and cannot identify any 'men of God' in your life who 'look out for you' - then I strongly advise you to ask Father to bring them into your life....

Starting Again

In January 1970 the Lord stepped into a situation in my life which basically caused me to start my relationship with Him all over again! Those who have read my first book: "The Turning of the Tide", will realise what I'm referring to. For those who haven't - let me explain. I came to the end of myself and attempted suicide - but God stepped in and caused a lady who was stone deaf to hear, and she got help in time to save me.

As part of my recovery my parents, in Germany at the time as my father was in the Army Fire Service, came and took me back with them to Germany. I found myself away from all believers - just me and God. I've always been so thankful for that, as it enabled me to start all over again and build a love relationship with Him that has lasted and in which I've just gone deeper and deeper.

I'm not saying all my muddled thinking was changed overnight but, through the years, I've learned to go to Him for the answers I need.

A Different Scenario

Around Easter of 1990 the Lord moved me in to live with a single Mum and her two remaining children living at home - a boy aged 9 and a girl aged 11. These were the two youngest of her eight children, having been married twice - and been divorced from both husbands. I was 46 years old at the time and, as you can imagine, my friend (we were good friends by then) was curious concerning the fact that I'd never married.

One of the things I shared with her that I regretted

was the fact that I'd never had children of my own; although I'd had a fair amount of contact with children through the years. She just looked at me and grinned - and said she had plenty for both of us which, of course, she did! Over the time we shared together, which was the following 25 years - I found I began to share responsibility within the family with their Mum, concerning their lives, etc.

Since their Mum went to be with the Lord in 2014, I've very much viewed them as part of my life and 'looked out' for them - both in the good and the difficult times. It's been a two-way situation as they've often come to me about things and also have helped me at various times also.....

It Worked For Me

I want to remind you here that what worked for me - wouldn't necessarily work for you; so please don't go looking for something similar. Remember, we are all created to be unique in the Family of God - and He treats each one of us as a separate entity and plans our lives to be what's best for us as individuals. That's why it's so important that we don't compare ourselves with one another, but accept that He created us to be as we are and that we are each one precious in His sight.

But for me 'it worked' - a fulfilled single life, with the company of a dear friend who also loved Jesus - and with children included!

On My Own Again

When I was on my own again at the age of 70, after my friend went home to glory - I found that Father had new plans for me. Please don't think your life is over because there are often a lot of changes when you're in your latter years. Let me say very clearly that there is NO AGE in the SPIRIT and God will use both young and old (and every age between) to build His Kingdom if we are willing to be used! And…. we really do need to remember that, whatever age we may be, we're not actually 'on our own' - we have Jesus with us and we're travelling on our journey of life with Him.

A New Season

I realised that my life was going to be very different from the previous 25 years, but believed, as my Father took me into a completely new season of my life, that He already had it planned out long before. I started going to the Blessing Church - relatively new in the town where I live but which, due to my friend being taken terminally ill with cancer, we'd not been able to attend when it first started.

Again, those who have read my first book will be familiar with how the Lord made me part of the church family there during the five years it was functioning in the town, and I eventually became the Pastor's PA! After it had closed, and with the onset of the pandemic, Pastors Joe and Josie (now living in the midlands), moved into a ministry online - which I'm also involved in and continue to be part of the Blessing Family.

Becoming A Writer

Amazingly, at least it's amazing to me, I began to start writing my first book towards the end of the first year of the pandemic. Pastor Joe, himself an author, is a much appreciated guide who helped me - just as he is helping me with this, my second book. This isn't the place to go into all the detail - but it's been quite a journey, and one that started many years ago.

The Story Behind This Book

As I've already shared - this isn't the place to explain more about how the first book came to be written. But I will share more about this one that you're reading! I shared some of it at the beginning of the first chapter, when I said I'd been asked the question in June 2022 - "Do you feel led to write something about your singleness, as an encouragement to others?" And I'll share with you now that it was Pastor Joe who asked me the question; and also the other question in October 2020 - "Did God ever reveal to you why your path did NOT include marriage and children?" I promised to share with you the answer I gave to him - once I'd got over the shock of his question!

This was my reply to Pastor Joe's question:

"I have to be honest - there was a time when I would have loved to have married and had a large family!! I think the Lord gave me the next best thing - a close friend and companionship.... along with a load of kids thrown in, who became like my own over the years!!!

Looking back now, I think I'd have to say that I'm not sure that, when I was much younger, I had the emotional stability to have coped with marriage and children. I'm not sure how else to explain it, but that's what came back to me, that I thought about at one point. It wasn't a 'clear Word' from the Lord but those are the thoughts I had. I think it was before I knew the friend I shared with - so I would have been in my 40's then...."

I also promised (at the beginning of the first chapter) that I would share with you the question I asked Pastor Joe resulting from his question to me! I asked him: "What had brought him to the point of asking me the question?"

This was Pastor Joe's response:

"Wow! Actually, God gave me a word for you about this, but I wanted to confirm it.... that's why I asked you. I will send it. You almost took words out of my mouth!"

I was 76 when Pastor Joe had this word for me:

"I prayed for you 27/10/20 and I heard the Father say, that I have been jealous over you since birth. You have never been alone.

You may have been single but I have always been there with you. I know you well and knew what was in your path. Being unmarried did not only make you different, it made you set apart. You have been happier single. You could have not been as happy as you are if you were married. I protected you from potential heartbreaks and marriage dramas that you could not cope with says the Lord. I did not allow a burden upon you that you could not handle. Whilst marriage has been a blessing to many, it has been a burden to many.

The Heavenly Father says the reason why I designated you to a life of singleness is for my purpose. I am your husband and you are still on course to give birth to amazing things in the Spiritual. There is still much for you to do! You have been set apart in your past so that you can move into Divine destiny for the rest of your life. As you gave me your singleness, I took it and used it for my glory says the Lord.

GOD BLESS YOU"

I saw it very much as the Lord's answer and explanation as to why He led me through my life as a single person - rather than being married.

'Whole' In Jesus

I trust that what I have shared in this book has given you some idea of my journey through my life as a single person, rather than having been married.

We have been created to be 'whole' in Jesus - and that is true whether we are married or single. It's the KEY to life for each one of us, and it doesn't happen overnight. In fact, I don't think our journey to the fulfilment of this actually ends until we're with Jesus in glory.

I think I have learned more about being made one with Jesus in the last few years - than I did in the previous 50 odd years. Be encouraged - He never gives up on any of us, but always wants to take us further forward in unity and in our love relationship with Him. Keep going deeper in your love relationship with Jesus.

Epilogue

Where To Now?

If you are single, and you have read this book in order to help you sort out what you really think about it all - I do pray that it may have helped clarify your thoughts; and hasn't confused you any further. I would encourage you, whatever your conclusion, to make sure you talk to the Lord about it and find out what He is saying to you personally…..

Get it Sorted Out

If you've got as far as this and are still not sure what exactly is the conclusion you've arrived at - I would say again: "Please talk to your Father about it." Don't just 'muddle' on - not knowing what you think or where you're going…..

Take the Challenge

If you have been challenged by what you have read - please accept the 'challenge' - and do something about it. Maybe read the book through again and see if you still feel the same way about it all. But my prayer is that you won't just leave it, but talk honestly with the One Who has the answer!

These first three paragraphs in the Epilogue arise out of, and basically deal with, what we've discussed through this book - "How to cope with being permanently single." And could also be of some help to those in widowed or divorced situations.

However, I would like to look briefly at one other situation…..

Single and Waiting!

Are you single at the moment and waiting for God to bring the right man / woman into your life with a view to marriage? How are you coping with the situation? What do you think you need to know going forward?

When I look back now, from my experience of walking with the Lord through many years, I think of what I would / should have wanted to have known in that situation…..

I have come to the conclusion that I would have

wanted to know the "Key to it All" which, as you probably realise is exactly what I wanted to know concerning being content and at peace with being single! The answer I came to was that ***Jesus needs to be Central to it All*** - and I believe that, in fact, is the answer to being 'Single and Waiting'.

I don't intend to leave you to work it all out for yourselves - but the answers to some of the following questions / statements require some ***homework*** being done on your part!

The Way Forward

I can't give you the answers that you might want to know, only you can provide those, but what I can do is pose some questions / statements to give you a framework to work on - to help you come up with some answers. Hopefully they'll give you some encouragement at the same time. You see I find very often that the answers to my queries come as I work through them and talk them over with the Lord - which is really what I'm urging you to do here....

Don't feel confined to the order I've put these bullet points into - we all work differently - so choose which order you want to tackle them in - you'll come up with better / more accurate answers that way. And I would suggest jotting down the answers, as well - and spend time talking to the Lord about them.

- **What is God saying and how do I trust Him?** This actually isn't only applicable to the area that we're looking at - it's true of any decisions we have to make! Tell God how it is for you, after all He knows already, and be **honest**. Don't rush it! And if you find it difficult to trust Him - say so. I really encourage you to spend time with your Father and let Him have the opportunity to let you know what's on His heart - and be willing to listen…..

- **What can I do whilst I'm waiting?** This is **not** the time to dwell on the 'waiting' and what you're 'waiting for' - but to concentrate on whatever the Lord has shown you to do and to keep on being obedient to that. Walk with Him through each day and deepen your relationship with Him - that's your part in it all. And that frees Him to do His part in working out what He's planned for you….

- **Dealing with the pressure.** I feel that this, actually, can be one of the really difficult and challenging areas of this time of waiting that is faced. I think it comes from two different directions - with the first coming, in fact, from yourself and is especially the case if you've been waiting for some time, and might have allowed your thoughts to dwell on what 'might be'!

The second direction it comes from is from your family and friends, whose expectations are that you will marry…. and aren't backward in saying so. In both instances you'll hopefully be aware that a lot of it is the enemy instigating it and feeding lies into your mind. That's when you need Father's help to change your mind-set and your heart attitude - away from the enemy's lies and back to what He is saying about your situation, remembering that we do have a choice as to what we think about and that He will help us. We don't have to do it on our own…..

- **Encouragement in the Situation.** Do you remember, how we're told in the Word, that "David encouraged and strengthened himself in the Lord his God." (1 Samuel 30:6). There will be times when you feel like giving up - that it's all too much. But that's the very time when you need to follow David's example - and encourage yourself in the Lord and let Him strengthen you. He is the only One who knows the 'end from the beginning' and He knows what He has planned for you in love. So turn to Him for His help and let Him take you forward, step by step…

I trust and pray, that these questions / statements will be of help in your time of waiting - and will be of encouragement to you.

But remember - ultimately, it's your relationship with Jesus, and keeping Him at the centre of it all - that will take you through this time.

Be richly blessed!

Printed in Great Britain
by Amazon

24373206R00036